THE ART OF
BEING
RECAPTURING THE SELF

Published in 2005 by
Stewart, Tabori & Chang
115 West 18th Street
New York, NY 10011
www.abramsbooks.com

Canadian Distribution:
Canadian Manda Group
One Atlantic Avenue, Suite 105
Toronto, Ontario M6K 3E7
Canada

Library of Congress Cataloging-In-Publication Data
is on file with the Library of Congress.

ISBN: 1-58479-405-4

Translated by Rosemarie Connelly

Designed by Lucile Jouret

The text of this book was composed in Bembo,
Gill Sans, and Caliban

Printed in France

10 9 8 7 6 5 4 3 2 1

First Printing

Stewart, Tabori & Chang is a subsidiary of

LA MARTINIÈRE
GROUPE

*To my son, for the wisdom
he inspires in me.*

THE ART OF
BEING
RECAPTURING THE SELF

CATHERINE LAROZE

CONTENTS

Introduction 6

SYNCHRONIZED MOVEMENT 8

Drifting Off 10

What Do You Do? 16

Childhood 22

Eclipse 32

Do 36

Keep Moving, at All Costs 42

The Garden 48

Scruples 50

The Downward Spiral of Happiness 58

The Train 66

In Hiding 68

REDISCOVERING YOURSELF 74

Do Nothing 76

Break Away 80

The Gardenia 86

Silence 88

Music 96

Solitude 98

Boredom 104

Laziness 112

The Dressing Gown 120

Idleness 122

The Armchair 130

Daydream 132

Become Yourself 138

INTRODUCTION

The art of doing nothing—of simply being? That sounds a bit like a provocation. And yet it's appealing, isn't it? It's as if the phrase doing nothing reminds us of something ancient within us—a manner of existing, of thinking, of behaving—that has been long forgotten but that we should call up from the depths, so that it seems familiar again.

Recall some relaxing moments from your past. A whole morning ahead of you, a beach stretching as far as the eye can see, trembling leaves in the autumn breeze, water sparkling beneath your feet. Imagine the feeling of days without end, of vacations that blend with everyday existence, of growth and a flowering of your soul, of a strong sense of freedom.

As positive and happy as these images are, they are also fleeting and often detached from everyday awareness. These thoughts seem to go against the grain of life; in fact they are directly opposed to our everyday rhythm. By thinking and experiencing them, we must temporarily renounce values to which we otherwise strictly adhere: efficiency, speed, action. . . .

Maybe you're saying, "Isn't it then unthinkable to dream of doing nothing, if I want to remain sensible?" Don't be so sure! Isn't it just a question of changing your point of view? Doing nothing: that need not mean literally resigning yourself not to act or not to do something; it might mean instead choosing another direction, committing yourself to a new path—one that is not so well marked.

You say it's not easy? Of course not. It's not easy to change everything about the way you act just by saying that you'd like to; it's not easy, and it's not even desirable for it to be that easy. The challenge is to make use of a new manner of being, to integrate the art of doing nothing into your practical life without renouncing everything that you've fought for, everything that you live for, everything that, despite all, continues to motivate you.

On the other hand, we have a lot to learn about doing nothing, a lot to learn about ourselves. In our single-minded quest for efficiency, we may find we barely know ourselves anymore. We have a lot to learn about our links with existence, about priorities, commitments, duties that we owe ourselves.

Learning to question certain habits, opening ourselves to laziness, boredom, and idleness—these are some ways we can attain the mindset of doing nothing as an art. We should envision the personal quest to attain this mindset as a privileged space where silence, tranquillity, and listening are open doors leading to the recapture of our own selves.

— Catherine Laroze

SYNCHRONIZED
MOVEMENT

Our minds are always racing; we're constantly on the run— faster, always faster; we're moving, traveling, and feeling as though we live a thousand lives in one lifetime, melting into the movement of the world and thus becoming part of a larger planetary motion. Always thinking bigger, higher, farther; but for all this mastery of time and space, have we mastered ourselves?

Drifting Off

Imagine yourself stretched out on a lounge chair under the shade of a tree, hands resting on a book. You let yourself go, eyes closed, while the scent of gardenias wafts past in soft waves. Your thoughts are vague and dreamy, a mixture of children's voices, birds' songs, and the mildness of the perfumed air. Suddenly a voice asks, "What are you doing?"

"Nothing."
"Nothing?"
"Nothing! I'm doing nothing!"

The situation is mundane. So is the question. We've all been asked it a hundred times, and we've asked the question of others as well. So why, at this exact moment, does it sound so bizarre?

It's because today, in fact, you are committed to doing nothing, and the question, instead of playing its normal role in routine conversation, falls flat. You are doing nothing. Absolutely nothing. Therefore you're forced to cut the conversation short—you have nothing to say.

Meanwhile, the questioner means no harm. He's showing interest in you, maybe even concern. It could even be the proof of love, tenderness,

friendship. But today, all this question does is annoy you.

It's almost as if you have to justify yourself to him.

Of course, you could say in a joking manner, "Yeah, I'm doing nothing today, I'm pampering myself, reveling in the moment. . . . I'm just wallowing here, and I'm not going to do anything all day, so do whatever you want, I'm just going to dream."

But you could never say all that in seriousness. Instead, to reassure yourself that you have the right to relax, you mentally go over all that you've accomplished since this morning to see if, according to some internal balance, you can authorize yourself to take a break: "I finished the work I had to do, the kids ate lunch, the laundry's hung out to dry, I made that phone call. . . ."

You realize that, though it may seem friendly, the question is intrusive, and perhaps the questioner is too. You feel yourself close up like an oyster, your sense of relaxation evaporates, and you suddenly feel obligated to defend yourself.

Are you being oversensitive? Is this a passing emotion? Not at all.

What you can learn from this relatively insignificant situation is that it is not very commonplace to do nothing; that is, to make time for yourself, to dream, to think, to listen to the stirrings of your soul. Also, you learn that it is difficult for others to accept that this is something natural and normal, an inner necessity.

The concepts of retreat, withdrawal, distance, of "doing nothing," all pose a fundamental problem today. Unless you are a hermit living in complete solitude, the fact of living as part of society, however limited this society may be, forces you to function in active mode. We are so integrated in society's interdependent network that it is almost impossible to extract ourselves from it, so that we may live for ourselves.

The question, What are you doing? or What do you do?—given that the person asking it is neither our boss nor our school principal—is in reality a complex sociological probe, full of insinuations about priorities and demands. These questions are instruments, albeit often used subconsciously, of a school of thought that hates to see us escape; like a slap, it forces us back to our ranks, implicitly forcing us to redefine ourselves and to put ourselves back in the context of social relations.

The air no longer seems as light, it loses its perfume— the cries of the children become irritating. You fall, despite yourself, back into the daily rhythm that never lets you escape. Apathy settles in. You realize that so much energy, so much willpower, so much determination to savor each instant of experience, are needed just to give you, each day, a reason to go on.

It takes so little to turn off the music of the world, for a laugh to die in your throat, for a tender moment to evaporate. The tenderness, the attentiveness, the willingness to take the necessary time that we can develop within ourselves can fall prey to the slightest brusque movement, to the slightest anxious thought. The smallest distraction can threaten our very sense of existence.

We have learned to work, think for, and abide by the rules of the society in which we live, but we have not learned to think or dream for ourselves. We no longer know what it means to take our time, let our spirits unfold, let our imaginations run wild.

It has become vital, not just for ourselves but for everyone's sake, to oppose this blind mechanical pressure with an intimate force, a subjective power, a ray of warmth.

It has become imperative that we resist. Draw from yourself all the hidden energy and strength you possess, and release all that is original, unique, weird, fantastic; you must throw all this in the world's face, you must rise up against and oppose the blind and inescapable pressure of society with a living force, a deep and beautiful laugh.

Why?

So that the expansion of thought, imagination, and subjectivity may triumph. So that all our voices, however anonymous and distant, can be heard. So that all the nuances and differences of an individual will stand out in a world that threatens to become intrusive. All the great movements and social revolutions and metamorphoses begin with intimate revolutions. You can start right here, on your lounge chair.

Stretch yourself out again. Cover yourself with the blanket that slipped to the floor.

You can close this book if you want and contemplate the foliage that sparkles against the light. You can listen to the little voice that approaches you, telling you about the sandcastle she made.

You can doze off. You can do all this, totally, completely, but with happiness.

What Do You Do?

Not one day goes by without hearing these questions.

"What do you do?"

"What does he do?"

"What does she do?"

It has become a reflex, an automatic reaction, so much of a tic that we don't even realize it anymore; it is sort of an all-purpose opening question that allows us to establish social or intimate relations.

A brush of the hand, a smile, a supportive glance, and the question leaps out, ready-to-use, so practical. It's something to throw out at another person when you want to know more about him, but don't know how to approach him or how to make contact. It's a tool, a convenient tool, neat, modern, foolproof.

We can imagine the question as a door that we open to someone, or a bridge put up linking two riverbanks, according to the distance that unites or separates the two people. The question is like an interactive medium permitting a spiritual exchange, since politeness and convention

dictate that the person who was asked the question now ask it in return.

And so it goes, feeding and greasing the machine. Those who were strangers have now formed a bond, all thanks to this superficial game that has nevertheless permitted the two to verify that they exist for each other and for society.

A tool, then.

But for what purpose?

If the formulaic question, What do you do? or What are you doing? doesn't bring a positive response at first, the question is asked again, more forcefully.

From the start, the question requires a response. You can't just ask it back to the person without answering it first. That would be too easy! Although maybe this would be the time to try, as that would emphasize exactly how superficial and superfluous the question really is.

But usually you feel obligated to respond.

Your questioner is interested in you! The least you can do is respond to the question.

Either you respond, "As you can see, I'm in the process of making a loom, I'm thinking about my next book, I'm in the middle of preparing a chocolate cake . . . ," letting the question lead to more questions, answers, discussions, exchanges . . .

Or you can take the question more generally.

"What do I do?"

The moment has come; seize the inspiration. Who hasn't hesitated at one time or another before answering? You search within yourself. You ask yourself. You wonder—just for a few tenths of a second—where is your answer going to come from? During this short time lapse, you attempt to evaluate who this person is that is asking, why he's asking (is he asking formally, or really interested?), and, considering the situation, what an adequate response might be.

"You mean, what is my job?"

"What do I do?"

This is what you hear yourself say, in order to buy time. A laugh, ridicule, a sarcastic comment, forces you to hesitate just when you were about to make the leap. This is why you don't have a prefabricated response, a standard answer, for this kind of question. The other person is still there, waiting for an answer to his question, his smile becoming more and more fixed. This is getting serious.

Okay, let's go.

"So, I'm an architect, a lawyer, a hotel manager, a judge, a writer, a butcher, a mountain guide . . ."

One thing you might notice right away is that when someone asks us, "What do you do?" most of us respond, "I'm a _____."

Of course, sometimes this question doesn't lead to this kind of answer, and the person responds by telling about all their particular interests, making reference to all their degree coursework and specific experiences. But more often, it's the simple, automatic "I'm a _____" that is blurted out. This kind of answer clearly shows how we label ourselves, identify ourselves with an activity.

The question of "doing," under these conventional appearances, actually expands much further. It's a manner of interrogating somebody, cutting straight to the essentials. How deeply it cuts depends on how the person being asked identifies himself, the degree of perceived similarity between who one is and what one does.

The significance of this question is ontological. It concerns the very nature of our being, not just our acts, deeds, and occupations. It disregards the boundary between self and the exterior world. It pries deep into our very souls, sometimes violently, without any of the etiquette that it pretends to have on the surface.

Why do we feel the victim of aggression? Why do we feel as though something intimate has been taken from us, as if this question touches the most deeply hidden secret part of ourselves?

Violence, violation. . . . The question of what we do can be about as gentle as a winch!

We must ask ourselves, Why does this question provoke such a reaction; why does it seem to cut so deeply?

This question has become central to our lives. It is no longer restricted to itself, to its own domain. It talks about who we are, it makes us talk about who we are, it breaks barriers, it creates them.

We now need to go back in time, to discover how we got to this point.

Childhood

We can easily imagine the dawn of a new world, unless it is the dawn of a new life. The sun rises with its pale light, leaves whisper in the trees, insects dance, new scents blossom, thoughts still sputter as the mind stirs, and innumerable questions overflow, all into this universe in which we are born.

"A child feels like the son of the universe when the human world leaves him alone . . ."
Gaston Bachelard

Our five senses are not enough to capture all of the emergent signals, sounds, and sensations that fuse together to press against the consciousness of a person awakening to the world. It's a constant discovery of each moment, an exploration of the world's abundance and the incessant movement of nature, of beings, and of the surrounding space.

So the antennae perk up; the ear is still freshly receptive to the softest sounds; the tongue discovers unknown flavors; the hands marvel at the velvety touch of a peach, or at the bite of a rosebush, and learn to hesitate before touching the thorns. The nose fills up with the scent of a rose, and becomes more refined when it plunges into a bunch of mint leaves. Everything a child sees, infinitely big or infinitely small, seems to spin a web of curiosity for him. A simple flower, an insect's tracks, a cloud with a shape interesting enough to capture his attention; all of these sensory stimulations allow him to break into a world where reality and his imagination work together, a universe

from which he will emerge curious, enriched.

The slightest thing causes this consciousness to unfold for a child—a ripple in the water, paint peeling on a wall. So many little things seize the imagination, things that will be stored and added to the child's bank of knowledge.

It takes time for all of these impressions to be organized, defining the contours of a surrounding landscape that has not yet finished revealing its mysteries. Weeks, months, years, are needed before all that he has perceived makes sense and becomes part of the bigger picture.

It takes not only time but space as well—space for desires to blossom, for arms to open wide, for the body to dance, for movements to flow, for the child to find an intimate harmony. It takes space for a spirit to take off, to go beyond the boundaries of the horizon, to attack the highest mountains, to be engulfed by the depths of the seas. An internal space is needed as well as an external space, and these two poles mingle until they can no longer be differentiated.

But calmness is still essential, silence and peace, so that all of these events, from the least significant to the most formidable, can take their proper place; so that beyond the noise, the tenderness of the world can be sensed; so that silence can develop into music; and so that words themselves can give way to the eloquent whispers of the heart.

This space, time, and silence belong to us. We posses them—they are engraved in the deepest part of us, as if they are a part of our very framework. We have experienced them time and time again, and we can even, with a little effort, remember when they first revealed themselves to us. Remember when, having clawed your way to the top of a tree, you marveled at the surrounding countryside; or when you realized the presence of time, inevitable, in the wrinkles of a grandparent's face; or when the silence of a sacred place allowed you to find your way into the peace of the world.

Childhood is an opening, a beginning. It's a time to sense, to perceive, to be welcomed. The smallest details become engraved in your consciousness, even the seemingly insignificant events: the silhouette of a loved one, the intonation of her voice, the softness of a pillow beneath your cheek, the cold touch of your metal bed frame, the smell of a gravel path in the early morning, the smell of a horse coming in from a walk, facial expressions, certain gestures, the weight of a word, a conversation.

Everything, childhood absorbs everything, without discrimination. It keeps, it stores, it stocks all of these minute details; only later will inventory be taken.

Childhood is a time of internalization. Who knows better than a child how to slip back into the dreams within, into the imaginary world that he has created? Who knows better than a child how to remove himself from a difficult reality to find a better world, forgetting his surroundings completely? A child does not exist for the exterior world. He is there—we can see him—but he doesn't always answer when we call. Maybe he is absorbed in some small task, a book, or he is in the

middle of carefully constructing something; maybe he is contemplating
the path of ants coming from and going toward a rock, or he is dreaming,
collapsed in the grass, his chin resting on his arms; or maybe he is sitting
on the edge of a low wall, his legs dangling, with an absorbed look on
his face, inventing a different life.

This game allows a child access to the depths of his being. Thanks
to it, he can explore the meanderings and labyrinths of the spirit;
he can throw pebbles to the bottom of his well to see how deep it
is, he analyzes the night in order to pierce its secrets, he goes
beyond the mirror, he discovers the hidden meanings behind
smiles, the troubles that haunt the beings around him, he sees
others' true colors beneath their masks.

And so childhood rings out . . .

Always pushing forward, a child knows the richness of silence.
He knows that at the heart of dreams, in the shadows, certain
voices make themselves heard. A child is rarely a rambler—he
knows the harm that words can do. But he also knows their
magical powers and charms. The stories he invents are bridges
linking reality and his imaginary worlds.

During all this time, a child comes into his own; he builds himself
little by little, becoming enriched, absorbing everything. Before
growing up in the world, he grows up within himself. What does he
do to accomplish all this? Nothing. He does nothing. Yet we can see that
his existence is one of abundance, growth, flourishing. . . .

And here we are, thinking that we have lost our keenness, insight, and sensitivity somewhere along the road, those things that at one time made us feel that we were being reborn every day. We blame the weight of everyday life, the responsibilities and obligations that encumber us. Little by little, we think, our spirit has deadened. Enthusiasm, curiosity, and boldness have been replaced by brooding, moderation, and fearfulness.

Our period of enchantment and discovery has become a lost paradise. Gone is the child's land of haloed light, grace, no worries, innocence, and freshness. A blessed time for everyone, a place for blooming of consciousness and the senses; all this has been lost. An idealized childhood is a time of sensations, feelings, sensuality. It's a time to venture and to open up, where each second gives birth to a new impression, within you, outside of you. It's a time of escape, thanks to the power of imagination, from your duties and obligations; it's a time of development, construction, and discovery.

We believe this period to be passed, finished, and definitively lost.

In idealizing it, we have made it inaccessible.

We view this period half compassionately, half condescendingly. Since then we have advanced. We have overcome obstacles, crossed rivers—we have experienced metamorphosis! We can barely recognize ourselves. But have we really changed that much?

What about the fits of incessant laughter that we still sometimes have, or those black moods that seem to throw us out of our own bodies, the feelings of intense frustration that bring us down, those sudden urges to close up within our shells, or the times when we stare aimlessly into space? Childhood continues in a thousand different ways within us. Our childhood pasts inspire the present, underpin our reactions, guide our choices, saturate our thoughts, direct our desires—all this despite ourselves, without us really being aware of its influence. Sometimes it's the joyful child within us who is speaking; another time it's the angry child who expresses himself; sometimes even the bored child who yawns.

Thus, childhood is never really over.

What we must do is draw out the little things from our childhood, the tiniest things that serve to support reverie and provide food for the imagination.

Seated on a step in the warmth of the June sun, chin resting on knees, you look at the small space between your feet. Of course, you are doing nothing, strictly nothing, but back in a time and a place since lost, you are experiencing, without doubt, one of the greatest feelings of expansion possible.

This childhood that exists within you gives you a chance to seize a living force, intact and unchanged in its expression. We should look upon childhood with the utmost kindness. This childishness is not at all ridiculous or reprehensible. It is an expression simultaneously of insanity and wisdom. Allowing your childhood to live within you as an

adult is, in effect, the sign of a spirit that is not completely willing to let itself be pulled into the exhausting whirlwind of adult life.

This is why we need to listen to the childhood that lives inside us— this part of us that continues to marvel, to pay attention, to be free. Instead of repressing it, constraining it, or worse, denying it, we should, on the contrary, give it room and welcome it as a precious new beginning, a time of learning. In this way we can secure a new manner of being, master the art of doing nothing, and free the circulation of our juices of life and energy.

To do this is to refuse to close your eyes, to put your hands over your ears, or to close your mouth. To do this is to keep the doors to your body and soul wide open. To do this is to let unfold a field of possibilities.

Eclipse

One day, you notice that a separation has taken place, a line has been crossed. Childhood is long gone, entrenched in the limbo of existence—inaccessible, foreign.

The change occurred progressively and smoothly; you barely noticed it happening. One day after another passed, each bringing new obligations and duties that accumulated and became intertwined, forming narrow, opaque walls around you.

Standing firmly on your feet, you take your role in this performance to heart, feeling pride in it. You participate in social life; you become a link in the network. Your actions become more effective, precise, your thoughts clear-cut. Your step has become rapid, your movements brusque. You are drunk with a different kind of power. Death does not exist for you. Laughter shakes you. Tears are not far from falling. But life is stronger than anything else, now.

You have made choices. You must at least accept that. You have made these choices in good faith, with enthusiasm even, like a brave little soldier, and now you must live with them. You made these choices

consciously and eagerly. Your mind is functioning perfectly, and you are physically at your peak, but meanwhile beneath it all you are uneasy; cracks are forming within you, and your energy is seeping out. So you begin to stumble from time to time. You find yourself lost on the road between childhood and adulthood. You thought you were made of iron, confident and certain, but suddenly, underneath your feet, the ground gives way.

Those old needs, questions, and repressed fears once again take hold of you, although you believed them to be long gone. You fall into the shadows of melancholy. You are drowning. But not for long—just long enough to take a breath of air, to glimpse forgotten images, and to come up to the surface in a great explosion of life, to strike once again at the fresh air, with movement, with all the strength of your body and the liveliness of your mind.

Moving and doing are the most important things in your life now. You build your life by acting, reacting. Your acts, decisions, and words contribute to a bigger project whose purpose, if it isn't obvious to you yet, is to pull you always forward. What counts in life is to advance. Being still now is the opposite of life; this is what you have been taught over the years. You must get up and get things done. Don't take your time; act, create, do projects, plan, experiment, stay awake, be always ready to *do*.

Doing has become like second nature. You realize this every morning. The moment the alarm clock rings, tearing yourself heavily from your dreams, you enter a new dimension, and you ask yourself if it is more real than the one you just left, because it seems so plastic-coated, so artificial. Immediately, the mechanical gears that you know so well are set into motion, causing a series of automatic actions that have become ritual, like second nature, each layered over the first until you can no longer distinguish them from one another. Thus your entire spirit conforms itself to this new manner of being. You have no choice. How can you fight against this invader?

Finally the struggle is over. The language, the words, the desires, fall silent. Unable to fight against this way of life, your body accepts it, even requires it now. The ringing alarm, the morning shower, the cup of coffee or tea, the world news on the radio, your hands on the steering wheel, book bag on your back, a door swinging open, a computer screen coming to life, meetings, telephone calls, the noises of machines, the roar of the drill—all of these things bite, stimulate, titillate, and excite your body, throwing you into gear, giving you the precious energy, the drive to move forward.

We need it. Our bodies need it, and our spirits too. It has become something necessary, like a drug. We know this. It's a stupefying drug that holds out the marvelous paradise of success, mastery, elevation, and reputation and makes you always crave more, as if you are in withdrawal.

This need has a name: *Do.*

D o

Do: this word is everywhere.

I do sports, I do the dishes, I'm doing the marathon, I'm doing . . .

The word is everywhere, to the point of making you sick.

It has become integrated in contemporary language, taking on a specific connotation, transforming activities, things, objects, or events into a product.

"A soul with no established goal loses itself."
Montaigne

Do: this word gives an action a slightly different meaning—the activity automatically seems more voluntary, more of a decision, more of a technique mastered; it's as if, by using this little word, we are looking to push aside any suspicion that something might happen by accident. The word even makes an action seem like more of a necessity.

To *do* something, you understand, is not a neutral concept. The use of the word has modified our way of looking at the world, and above all, our manner of existing in the world. To do something actually suggests that we have mastered or wish to master the thing that has been done. As we use this word, we show our demands to the world. The word induces a demand.

To *do* something, in a way, is to place the activity at a distance from yourself; to consider it a dissociated activity, boxed in, limited. The activity becomes a consumable product, we have the right to demand from it a certain standard, a certain amount of satisfaction.

I do the cleaning. My cleaning must be perfectly done. I demand it. There's no room for chance, for imperfection. My cleaning must correspond to the archetypical cleaning job—the ideal cleaning, a cleaning job so perfect, it could appear in *Home* magazine.

Our obsession with mastering things seeps into a number of domains, particularly those that are dependent on randomness or chance. These anxieties thus plague even our leisure activities and vacations. The way we use the word do creates a tendency to discount the role of chance, luck, happenstance. People who "do" Mount Blanc intend to accomplish the hike based on previous impressions, learned ideas that they have built up in their heads, or that someone proposed to them. But the reality often clashes with these preconceptions.

We have the impression that we can no longer dream about or imagine our trips. People "do" trips; they "do" Egypt, for example. The word implies that there exists one correct way to travel, to look at things, to enjoy ourselves.

What is lost when we approach traveling like this are our feelings of freedom and discovery, of experiencing the unplanned, the unforeseen, all of which are appropriate when we explore a new country. But now everything must be regulated, thought about, mastered—above all, it must stick to the plan; changes and last-minute modifications are very unwelcome to those who prefer something more precise.

So "doing" is linked with spending—spending energy and money. We demand results because today we feel that everything is prefabricated, and everything—pastimes, free time, alone time, freedom—can be bought.

If everything can be bought, than everything must be profitable.

If I go on vacation, it's to "recharge my batteries." If I travel, it's for a change of scenery. If I visit a museum, it's to become cultured. If I go for a walk in the morning, it's to get some fresh air. If I work out, it's to prepare myself for the ski season. If I go on a diet, it's to look good on the beach. If I climb the highest mountain, it's to "do a first." If I play soccer, it's to give me a sense of team spirit. If I win money . . .

We can never do something for no reason. Everything must have a reason, be useful, justifiable.

Exit pure enjoyment. That is, exit the beauty of movement, for ourselves, for the pleasure of it, for the sake of it. No longer can we take naps, walk, or read just for its own sake.

We are always worried about mastering things, from our tiniest acts to the deepest parts of our psyche.

Childhood, dreams, free time, vacation, old age, crazy thoughts, rest . . . all

must serve some purpose.

The issue of doing is no longer restricted to itself. It has taken on a larger significance. It flows over into all aspects of life, dreams, liberty, imagination, thought, even spirituality; it has taken over all aspects of our being.

Doing carries such weight today that it has become a substitute for being; the two have fused together. Doing has become a touchstone, a horizon to anchor the landscape of being.

Keep Moving, at All Costs

Quick! Quick! Run! You're hurtling down the crowded boulevard. Are you going to be late? Not at all. You just can't waste time dodging traffic. Your technique? It's been tried and tested over the years. You look at a landmark in the distance—a lamppost, perhaps. Then you charge at it. The most important thing is not to deviate from that straight path, not to stray from the line you are following.

"The man of the world hides entirely behind a mask."
Jean-Jacques Rousseau

Your speed is fine-tuned: hands in pockets, chin jutting forward, your step large and ample. You find a rhythm, fall into it, and perform each movement as an expression of a forceful decision. This determination has imposed itself upon you, and now you impose it upon others.

You walk rapidly. You dig through the crowd before you; you are parting people as the bow of a ship parts the waters. You actually enjoy the feeling that the world is moving around you, because of you, according to your wishes. Sometimes you recognize someone like yourself. Same determined step, same purposeful movements. Suddenly, like a puff of air, you meet. But two trains traveling at the same speed have no effect on each other.

Most people, on the other hand, hesitate around you. You can see them walking slower and slower until finally they stop. When you reach them, they dive abruptly to the side to let you pass. You wonder how long it must take these people to reach the end of the boulevard.

Two minutes and forty seconds. The record has been broken. Whose record? Yours, of course. There's no other witness. The record is for your own pleasure. It's a glorious, intimate victory. There's no use in running clumsily, you know this well. You are only interested in the euphoric feeling brought on by your streamlined speed, performance, and efficiency. It's a way of testing yourself, to see if you are really up to the bar that you've set for yourself.

It's also a way of measuring others, not only to see if you are their equal, but also to see if you can surpass them, be competitive, be the leader of the pack.

Tiring? Yes, it is sometimes. It's impossible to be permanently hard at work. You need to breathe, take a break, save some energy to start again later. Between these moments of euphoria and of action, you need to "drop your mask!"

Drop your mask? What mask?

Your mask! Moving, doing, at all costs; it's you, yet it's not you. The days that you feel full of go and in possession of all your energy are paradoxically the same days that you are faced with doubt, as if, having arriving at the very peak of a mountain, you've discovered that the surrounding landscape is completely featureless.

A strangeness—something just isn't right.

Your face, your features—okay, it's definitely you. Your hair, all your little details, you recognize with no trouble. But there's something else, something that holds and animates your face. This something is not a hard, opaque mask; it's more subtle than that, like a facial expression or the attitude you carry. An expression or an attitude that is not natural to us, in which we look for ourselves without success.

Do you remember the curiosity with which you looked at your own face at the beginning of adolescence? It was then that this intimate quest began, the quest to question your character, to discover the secret meanings of your existence. If your face seemed mysterious back then, that's because life itself was mysterious.

But today, it's a matter of something else. The mystery has disappeared, buried deeply, replaced by strangeness.

You don't know anymore where the "I" is in your face. In vain you search for it—it should be clear, readable. It used to appear sometimes, revealing itself in some places only to vanish in other places.

Where am I?

This is what you ask yourself when, out of breath, you stop. Where am I in this movement, where am I in this activity, in this never-ending race?

But be honest! How many times have you allowed yourself to stop and ask these questions? Of course it has happened, but haven't you just gotten into the habit of avoiding it? Haven't you fallen into the habit of not recognizing yourself? Haven't you become a stranger to yourself?

Do you really know yourself?

And in running so fast, isn't it only from yourself that you are escaping?

The Garden

Sheets of paper, pens, and ink are in place. Books are open, the documents are ready, the cup in your hand is filled with a steaming brew. Everything is there, as usual, just as it is every morning. But despite all, your mind is in the clouds. You tried changing your position, adjusting the thermostat, unplugging the phone, getting up and sitting down, rubbing your worry stone . . . but there's no sense in forcing it.

You never doubted that one day or another, this would happen. A breakdown, a real breakdown. A stupor, a daze, astonishment! You don't even know what to call this paralysis that is constraining you right now . . . too many things, too much of everything. Nothing manages to reanimate your face, to wake up your energy, neither your favorite books, nor your familiar portraits, normally harbingers of hope and constructive ideas. . . .

But even as you give up hope, a soft breeze caresses your face. A draft, no doubt, seeping in through the windowpanes. A breath of tender grass, fresh water, and mossy stones.

Outside, to the garden! It is there, just a few yards from you, and yet you no longer see it, you have been so blinded by daily tasks. It is there, pale and slightly trembling in the white light of early morning. You throw

a sweater over your shoulders and quickly go down the stairs. The
door resists a bit—the wood is swollen.

Timidly, you advance. The garden's austere naïveté moves you. It
is a child, yet old at the same time. It never stops growing new
shoots, all the while becoming deeper in its old age. You have
walked its pathways before, but today you are seeing it for the
first time. How could you have forgotten? Quickly, you evaluate
the work that needs to be done: pluck the grass from the paths,
remove the moss, trim the hedges, give order to the groups of
plants, cut dead branches, tie back the rosebushes . . . there are
so many things to do.

But the garden is beautiful as it is. A little abandoned, a little
crazy. Slightly rambling. It speaks of a life that lets itself go
tenderly, of emotions that pour out freely, of sensations that know
no restraint. A carnation—how is there a carnation growing in
this season?—exhales a soft scent, like a sigh.

What are we afraid of, that we want to put everything in order?

Pensive, you sit down on a stone bench. A ray of sunlight licks your
cheek. You remove your shoes and caress the earth with your bare feet.

Scruples

Running . . . running . . . but something, or rather someone, catches your attention.

A man is there, pacing in front of a store. He is dressed in an overcoat, a suit, and a tie. His shoes are well polished. In his hand he holds a slim leather briefcase like that of a professor or doctor. Periodically he looks at his watch, preoccupied; his appointment is late.

But this man isn't waiting for someone, and nobody comes to meet him. Those who take this route daily know that each day he can be found in front of this store window, pacing back and forth for hours, pretending to wait for someone.

It's the repetition of his action that makes it bizarre; without it, you wouldn't find anything strange about this man—except maybe, if you looked carefully, something feverish and worried in his eyes.

The situation is ordinary, terribly ordinary. It's only fair if it elicits feelings of compassion from the people who know the truth. A man who has lost his job continues to make himself believe that he is still active, that he still has meetings, appointments, and projects. Maybe he says every morning to his wife, "See you tonight!" Maybe he hopes every

day to meet someone who can change his situation, or for an improbable event to occur.

An ordinary case, of course—you've seen worse—yet this man himself is a symptom. A symptom of a malady that any of us could fall victim to one day or another, which results from the tension caused by the constant injunctions to which we are subjected from the first days of our existence. "Do, work, never be still" could be the leitmotif of our era, with its quickened tempo of life—the creed of modern times, replacing individual free will.

You have to keep active! Doing is better than doing nothing. This way of thinking, if it is not to grind to a halt and provoke a total collapse, must justify itself. How many times have you heard, "You're not doing anything? Oh, good, do something, anything, occupy yourself!" You must occupy your time; you must do something. You cannot do nothing.

And so the man in front of the building keeps going. Even though the original purpose and reason behind his movements and actions has disappeared, he doesn't stop. Something inside him cannot give in to inactivity. He feels obligated to repeat the same actions, to play over and over the same scenes, and thus to participate in the movement of the world.

Or else what?

Or else he'll crack up, completely break down.

This man is trying, despite everything, to hold the pieces together; he is attempting, through this charade, to stay in sync with the world, keep up with the restrictions that he has pledged himself to. How long can this show go on? Impossible to say. But the whole thing resembles a house of cards, at the mercy of the slightest breath of air.

The man is fragile, he is troubling to us, his situation touches us. Beyond the human problem that he has fallen victim to, his behavior strikes a chord in us. Certain elements of his behavior, taken alone, are mundane, even familiar, but all the little compulsive signs, when put together, signal a significant problem.

We can all catch ourselves in these little compulsive behaviors: getting dressed up when we have nothing to do, looking at our watches when we aren't waiting for someone, and all those other things like consulting our agenda every five minutes, compulsively checking the answering machine. We put so much energy into occupying all the free time in our days.

In fact, we are all conforming, subconsciously, to this vast and universal movement that is permanently urging us to hasten our step, constantly pushing us into the near future, beyond the present moment. This movement, by definition, rejects the ideas of immobility, resting, the here and the now; this movement is mobility, stretching, motion, a push toward the future.

This movement creates a world where nothing is stable or fixed. It offers us an ever-shifting, evanescent view, like the view from a train traveling at top speed. The scenery changes continuously; by the time we

arrive at a certain point, it's already gone. Because of this movement, what we think we can touch is already somewhere else, thanks to the obligation to continue pushing forward. Landmarks have an extremely short life span, and this pressures us to constantly keep in step; if we fall behind, if we step aside and reject this headlong journey, the wind of the passing train could blow us away. Thus we keep moving too.

Even when we can reasonably stop, because we've finished our work, because we're tired, because it's vacation, because we need a break, because our schedule dictates it, or even because of some outside force (the weekend, job loss), we dare not. We don't even know how to stop.

This controlling force makes us continue to adhere to it, even when it is not useful. We continue to run, even when no obligation exists; we continue to be irritated and annoyed, even when nothing is nudging us; we continue to be on the alert, because we have to.

This need to do is what connects the outside world and ourselves. We believe that living on the go, in a constant state of excitement, juggling a thousand projects, is the hallmark of a particularly successful individual, active and energetic, functioning at his prime. This is because, while we are pushing forward, we are conforming to an exterior model that reinforces a positive, energetic, dynamic image.

The need to constantly "do" pulls at us from two directions, from within us and from the outside, where our society constantly reinforces the validity of our choices, of the direction taken. We are not capable of stopping; even our interior self is powerless to resist, because it in itself is obeying the exterior force. It's not just a question of one part of us adhering to this movement. What is required is our active, dynamic part. But there also exists other parts of us that only want rest, comfort, and inactivity. Imagine that one day we just stopped. What do we fear; what would happen?

It's not certain that we can interrupt this impetus with a simple choice on our part. The machine continues to turn, even without a precise purpose. It behaves like some mechanisms—better to keep it running on empty than to stop it. Similarly, we know that the world itself continues to advance. That's the reason why, even when we can stop, we don't.

This world in action, which will never run out of fuel or hit the brakes on its inexorable progression, sends us back all the more empty. It is difficult to oppose the enormous energy expended by the mechanical world in motion with the inaction of one individual. We prefer to stay afloat, even if sometimes we get overwhelmed by the current, even if sometimes we are forced to simulate movement—just a few token actions—in order to continue to be part of the greater movement, in order not to be left stranded on the banks.

This energy-saving technique can't last. Sooner or later you have to step up the tempo, make up lost time so that, once again, you can be active, swim in the same rhythm, carried by the stream, struggling against the current to be sure that you don't slip away, that you keep your head above water.

The golden rule for steering a small boat, we have learned, is to go faster than the current does. Thus we can avoid being at the whim of the waves, we can cut through turbulence, and we can find ourselves always at the crest, victorious, triumphant. We don't know where we're going, but we're going there, every one of us.

Intoxicating, euphoric, this great and beautiful human movement.

The Downward Spiral
of Happiness

You've left behind the man with the feverish look in his eyes. Your gaze slides across shop windows offering tableaus of seduction for compulsive buyers.

"You have everything, but you need more," says the vast array of well-placed goods behind the thin glass windows, touched by your eyes, almost touched by your hands. "You have everything you need, we know; you can live in peace without buying anything else—but come on, see what we have to offer you!"

Perhaps nobody is truly fooled, neither the consumers nor the merchants, big or small, but it's the law in the game of business. You have to make people want your product by making them feel dissatisfied when they see something extremely desirable that they do not have; your product must displace the topmost desire in their hierarchy of desires so that they have the impulse to buy your product, *now*.

This emptiness, this blank, that's what we must fill. This dissatisfaction, our little addiction to the dream of complete satisfaction, does not allow us to rest. We must once again find a feeling of plenitude, a way to justify to ourselves why we are constantly moving, working, and doing.

What's the point of running, exhausting ourselves, if at the end of the day we can't at least say to ourselves that we've reached our goal, that we've obtained what we desired, or that we're about to obtain it?

The double pleasure of satisfaction and movement is what gives sense to our lives!

We have to justify our constant movement. We have to justify our desire to be perfectly satisfied. Thus we let ourselves be seduced by the song of the sirens. We prick up our ears.

The sirens sing loud and strong. They don't hesitate to invade our existence. They are there to create a never-ending, never-satiated desire. From the moment we wake up, they strike up their song, pursuing us everywhere, leaving us alone only at night when we sleep.

And what do these sirens promise that makes us, despite all our precautions, listen to them so attentively?

They promise us happiness, paradise on earth, unending joy, balance, harmony, serenity. . . .

They know how to catch us, these delicious sirens.

And to do all that, to reinforce the power of their songs, they don't hesitate to use any means necessary: they splatter the pages of magazines with mouthwatering images and propositions; they stretch out in large format on billboards or on the curved subway walls; they serenade, repeating their refrains; they shine their bright lights in our eyes; they write words of desire in the sky.

But what does it all boil down to? Very ordinary things: cars, trips, clothing, accessories, watches, perfumes . . . but the way the sirens sing makes these objects seem like a haloed extension of the soul, artificial of course, but enough to pull the wool over our eyes.

Have we become that gullible?

No. Simply, we need to believe in something, and especially in this.

We need to give purpose to this race without a finish line, this race that has become a quest; we need inspiration for our continuous movement.

In order to live, we need sparks, rainbows, gold dust, rays of sunshine, lightning, ribbons, bubbles, smiles and laughter, warm winds, heartbeats, dizziness, tears, tension, shocks, aspirations, wishes, deliriousness, fantasy . . . everything that represents life for us, the essence of existence. And the sirens know it.

So there you go, it's a game that everyone indulges in, soullessly, since it's just a game!

A car with tinted windows, leather seats, a dashboard of shiny elm, gliding as an immaculate robe glides noiselessly across marble floors, detached from earthly events. On board are a man and a woman driving, not at all in a hurry, toward the unknown. It's us, yet it's not us. We believe in it, yet we don't.

But you must make yourself believe in what you believe.

This is the trap of the seduction. You know there are strings attached, you can see them with the naked eye; they are tried and tested, worn. And yet you dive in, with all your clothes on. This car, you absolutely want it. You will not rest easy until you have your hands on the wheel, until the kids are in the back seat eating cookies.

You can only see the bright side that comes with the car: liberty, freedom, luxury, independence . . . lulled by the sweetness of the image, you let yourself get taken away by cozy, sunny, stereotypical dreams. . . you imagine yourself someplace that is just pure fiction.

You are the man behind the wheel of the luxury car; you are the family on vacation by the edge of the pool or the transparent sea; you are a seductive woman idly prowling the city streets; you are the mother of a family, perfectly organized in front of your new stove; a high-performance athlete who always wins; a blue-eyed, salty-skinned sailor; an elegant, beautiful, successful manager. . . .

And at the same time, you are someone who runs around all day, answers the telephone with arms full of groceries, has words with the butcher who forgot your order, gobbles up artificially flavored candies against the rules of your diet, drops the entire contents of your work files in a crowded subway, snaps at the children. . . .

We navigate; we slide between dream and reality.

Fantasies enter into real life, and events that have really taken place recur in

our dreams. The boundaries are fuzzy, and fantasy and reality mingle more
and more frequently.

And the sirens continue to sing, their song resonating from televisions
everywhere, while everyone dreams of his hour of glory, of his slice
of paradise, and money floats in waves on dazzled winners of a game
of chance.

We live today as in the time of fairy tales. Big bad wolves are no
longer confined to the world of nightmares but live and breathe
in the cities; the worst catastrophes possible have become real; each
of these events shapes another; the virtual is reincarnated as reality.

And the sirens continue to sing, even if their same old song starts
to sound funny, even if their voices start to make you wince.

Sometimes you just don't have the heart to play anymore. Is it
weariness, lethargy, melancholy, or depression, as we discussed before?

You don't really know. It's nothing tangible, really. It's like a hair on
the clear crystal of existence, a scruple, but it's enough to bother
you and take away your appetite for life. In your mouth you taste
a light bitterness, an excess of saliva or of bile. An uprising, a
resurgence, a return to repression?

A feeling of disgust creeps in. The magic isn't working anymore. You no
longer have this impulse, this innocence that usually allows you to cling to
the tales, believe in the beautiful images that are presented to you. You have
dropped out. It's like a hangover, a sick headache, depression after the party.

You attempt to perpetuate the magic, but the whistle has been blown on this game. Nothing, no new idea, no new project, can pull you together. You are scattered. Your body and your spirit are in pieces. Beside you, the telephone rings, but you don't answer. Books are closed, their austere covers staring at you, and even vacation plans leave a strange taste in your mouth.

The Train

You finally sit down in your seat by the window. On the foldout table, your laptop, some books, and a newspaper are poised. You are waiting for the train to depart, cheerful already because these few hours of tranquillity give you the opportunity to work without being disturbed.

You still feel the trace of a vague emotion, an emotion that always rises to the surface when you cut through the crowds to catch the train and you smell fresh tar and hot metal—you don't even know if it's real or a figment of your imagination—a mixture of frenzy and suspended animation that occurs only in train stations.

But the feeling quickly fades as the shelter of the train car, like a monk's cell, works its magic, and you calm down. Of the outside world, you perceive only rushing silhouettes, and when the train noiselessly detaches itself from the platform, you're already elsewhere. You can finally get down to your work—even if you know that you'll have to fight against the almost hypnotic state induced by the even temperature, the subdued lighting, the faraway countryside, like an abstract behind the tinted windows, and the gentle rocking motion.

So why do you resist it? Because you don't have a lot of time, and it would be a shame to waste it. You open your book, you peruse the pages, sometimes reading the same sentence several times without retaining it. The train's own magic is taking hold of you. Your spirit follows this linear road, the tension between two points—your departure and your arrival—opening up freely to any possible chain of events between them. Between the place we leave behind and the place we're going extends a free space that allows the spirit to delve within itself, seeking events that decide one route or another.

And while the train rolls on, your thoughts stretch, expand, and bring you far from this carriage to a huge sorting station, which resembles existence itself.

In Hiding

A glance to the right, a glance to the left, and you're on the street. Your collar turned up, you glance around one last time to reassure yourself that nobody saw you leave.

Have you committed a crime, or are you to blame for some sin that you have to flee like this, without anyone noticing you? No, you haven't done anything against anyone. You are simply about to steal some time.

You couldn't let this opportunity go by. It was too perfect. So you seized it. Without saying anything, obviously. Lone rider. Time is like a stolen kiss, ripped away from existence. You're still shivering. Like a child pretending to be scared.

And now you walk—it's more like melting—through the streets of the city. You move lithely, but not too fast. You dare not let yourself go completely. The weather is beautiful, there's no humidity; children are out to get some fresh air in their strollers, the passers-by amble on apparently without any purpose, and there is a general worry-free feeling in the air.

You could have left in a different manner. But you are incapable of

exclaiming, "Okay, I'm done for today, I'm going to the movies and to see an exhibit." Or even better, "I'm going out for a stroll, with my hair in the wind." Meanwhile your coworkers, like schoolchildren, are working hard, hunched over their desks. You are not just reluctant telling others of your escape; you can't even admit it to yourself.

But what are you afraid of? How it reflects on you? You're really not sure. Perhaps Big Brother is watching you. You feel like a deserter, running from the scene of a crime. While other people are working away to pay their debts, you grab your bag and rush out toward the unknown, disappearing into nature.

The sharp, energizing smell of freshly cut grass stops you in your path. Unmoving, eyes closed, you breathe the air deep into your lungs. Is it the beginning of spring? It's a bit early, but why not? We should welcome the signs of the season to come: lightness in the air, a certain transparence, unusual vibrations.

You come to a gardener cleaning his clippers. Why are you gawking at this man? You haven't come very far, but you're already in zoned-out mode.

Hurry up, you have so little time! How often does it happen that you can wrench yourself away from your obligations? Honestly, you can count the times on one hand. You have trouble escaping. Always conscious-stricken, weighed down by feelings of guilt. Even when you go on vacation, even if you deserve it, you manage to waste it.

"Yes, yes, I'm leaving on vacation, I have to go . . . but obviously, you can still reach me. Don't worry about that. I have on hand, dear colleagues, the most subtle and modern means of communication so that twenty-four hours a day, seven days a week, whether I'm at the ends of the earth, on a desert island, at an intersection in Tokyo, in my grandmother's garden, or in a therapeutic mud bath, you will always be able to reach me.

"I will not leave you.

"Also, I will contact you to reassure you that I am still motivated, invested, and responsible. I've brought several files with me. A few days of rest will do me well so that I can look at them with a clear mind.

"I don't want to leave you.

"I'm leaving, but it's only so that I will be even more efficient when I return. You will not complain that I am gone, but rather you will reap the benefits when I come back. My vacation will benefit the team, it will be useful. . . .

"I'm afraid to leave you.

"I'm afraid that you'll leave me."

There, that's it. You're afraid that the cord, once cut, can never be mended. You're afraid of being left out at sea, stranded on a desolate bank, while the others continue to advance. You're afraid that you'll never again be able to catch up.

It happens so fast! So say those who watch the stream go by and hold themselves back from jumping in. See what happens if you continue to do nothing? The early bird catches the worm—and so on.

So your guilty conscience prevents you from enjoying what should be quiet and carefree moments.

While you're dawdling in town, it's as if a thorn suddenly hits you in the heart, and you jump. What about that file that needs to be finished tomorrow? You haven't even begun working on it yet. No, no, no! You must resist the pressure.

And to give more weight to your decision, you buy your ticket to the movie and slide silently into the dark room.

REDISCOVERING
YOURSELF

A partially opened window looking out on the garden, a lovely scent you breathe in, an early-morning escape full of promises, a child held tight close to your heart . . . it takes very little to bring you to a more intimate dimension and to experience the flowering of forgotten sentiments and sensations, bringing you closer to your true self.

Do Nothing

"Do nothing?

"Impossible!

"To do nothing for a weekend, or a few days—why not? But to do nothing at all, that is something I just cannot envision!"

"Doing nothing is easier said than done."
Raymond Devos

Who is speaking? Us, them, you . . .

Who has not said these words at one time or another? Where were you when these words were said?

If you were at the peak of your most active, dynamic, energetic mode, then yes, everyone agrees: to do nothing is hell. Precisely, to do nothing is a negation of all that you've done, of the energy and tension that you have endured to earn a sense of an active life.

In fact, from your regulated, organized, structured existence—where each instant corresponds to a specific activity and where emptiness is tracked down and each void immediately filled—you cannot imagine doing nothing without becoming filled with terror.

Just imagining "idle hands" makes you panic.

Your "active" life is actually a succession of tasks to accomplish that give your day a sort of framework. From the moment you get up to the moment you lie down at night, the events of your day, which consist of duties, problems, and worries, are viewed as obstacles to overcome, the resolution of which is key to your existence.

You must always look for ways to advance, build, create. People are programmed to move forward, and any pause in the motion is viewed as a sort of check.

"Doing nothing," strictly speaking, therefore has no place in this logic; it makes no sense.

Time that is not spent accomplishing something is viewed as "dead time," with no reason for its existence; it's not viewed as a pause that can restore the energy and vitality so necessary to us. The first thing that we do when we have this "dead time" is to immediately fill it up with the first chore that comes up, or, if we're well organized, with a chore that has been saved for this rare occasion of down time.

Organizing the closet, for example, is one of the unimportant activities that we leave for moments when we have nothing else to do. The act of putting away your things is a satisfying activity in itself, calm, neat; it allows you to reflect on the world, on your past, your present, the time that is now passing.

Often we hear, "When I have a spare minute I water the garden, do odd jobs, I take advantage of my free time . . ."

The fear of emptiness dominates people's lives.

Emptiness is a hole that could drain away all our useful energy; it is essential to plug this hole up.

Break Away

You got what you wanted. You were warned: you'll last two days, tops.

Emptiness surrounds you. The house is silent. The telephone hasn't rung, but it is working—you just checked. You never know.

This isn't some lab experiment, but something completely "normal": you are alone in a house for one week. The village isn't far away, and you can hear the noise of the highway; the car is available, so you can leave if you want to. You have music, books, work, paper, ink, and a computer all within arm's reach . . . no reason to worry.

But still . . .

A whole week—that could be long. Especially when you have nothing concrete to do, no project to hand in, nobody waiting for you.

You are surprised to find that in preparing for your week in the house, you packed a thousand useless things, as if all of these objects are charms to protect you from boredom, loneliness, and silence.

Once inside the house, you are your usual self. Incapable of sitting still for the first few hours, you give yourself a tour of the house, opening all the

closets, examining the drawers, inspecting the secrets of all the little boxes, gliding your hands over the piles of sheets, dreaming in front of the cupboard of fishing gear.

The very first thing you do is take off your watch, and then you put it back on your wrist almost immediately. Let's not go overboard. After all, this experience doesn't all come down to your watch.

A glance in the mirror reassures you of your good intentions. You're not crazy, no, not unreasonable, although it's true that a mountain of work is waiting for you while you are going to spend a week "doing nothing."

It's not a bet, nor a pride thing. You've simply decided to take a break because it seemed necessary. Reactions to your plan are mixed. Those who know you doubt that you'll be able to do it. But do they know what you're looking for? Do you know what you're looking for?

Wearing the landlord's hat, you leave the house to visit at the garden. Once again, you have a look at all the nooks and crannies: you inspect the flower beds, the thickets, the undergrowth, the vegetable garden, the fish pond. You pluck two or three withered flowers, tighten a tap that was dripping, then rush toward the outbuildings; there, in the dark and the dust, empty rabbit hutches and a stable await their guests.

You observe your surroundings: the color of the sky, the perfume of the wallflowers. Your feet crunch on the gravel, and then you return to the silent,

echoing house, where the only sound is the ticking of the old clock. You've
done all this once, twice, and now you feel like you're walking in circles.

You think of all that you've left behind in the "real world," the laughs,
the tears, life. Your reflection in the window stares out at the lonely
garden. The sigh that you exhale from the depth of your lungs is
unusually strong. Where did it come from? It doesn't seem to be a
sigh of regret, but, despite everything, more like a sigh of relief.

Relief? Of course, why not? You are really benefiting from this
week of relaxation.

Seated on a threadbare armchair, you take a book from the top of
your pile. The subject, as usual, is one that you are passionate
about. That's why you chose it. But now something holds you
back. The cord that links your thoughts and your interests has
been cut, and the words on that page dance and make faces at
you. Your attempt to concentrate on this book is in vain, and it's
useless to force yourself: the book slides from your hands, without
your even realizing it.

What are you doing?

Nothing—that's exactly it!

Still seated in the armchair, you listen more carefully to the clock.
You follow the swing to and fro of the pendulum. In the silence of the
house, each noise takes on a strange, stimulating, hypnotizing presence.
Naturally, your pulse and your breathing become part of its rhythm, and

you experience a soothing, relaxing sensation.

A dog barks. Someone calls out. You jump up like a spring, like an excited child. A curious neighbor has come to ask if you need anything, or if he can do anything for you. No, he can't do anything for you, you think with a hint of regret, nothing at all.

The man leaves, and as a beggar attacks food, you glean the hints of his presence: the smell of his hunting vest, of his pipe, and of his dog, his canine twin. And then in a few minutes, you are filled once again with your own solitude.

Wandering around the house, you rub your hands together vigorously. You suddenly feel determined to do something, but what? You're practically giggling out loud! "Okay," you hear yourself say in the austere silence of the house. What if you sang a little song? Your voice echoes, uncertain, ridiculous, absurd. Once again it falls silent.

It's probably the first time you've ever experienced such a thing. You feel like writing down your vivid impressions. Your notebook is there, blank, resting on the table in front of the garden window; you've prepared it for this purpose. "A poignant account of my experience, a true anecdote!" But nothing, absolutely nothing, comes out of your pen. Not even a few sentences that sometimes help you get on the right track, like singing exercises to warm up the singer.

Nothing. You've run out of gas.

Deprive the most modern and beautiful machine of oil, and it will jam up. . . .

All of this happens in just a few moments. Almost without realizing it, you grab the keys to the car, quickly stuff a few things in your bag—you'll come back later for the rest—close the door behind you, and open the gate to leave.

But at the last second, you turn around. Something holds you back.

The Gardenia

A flash. A presence. An aroma drifts in, arrestingly powerful. Then it's gone, almost as quickly as it came. Instinctively, you sweep the room, trying to discern where it came from, but nothing seems to have been the cause. Was it a mirage? Maybe. Sometimes, in thinking about a scent, you imagine that you actually smell it. But just now, it seemed real. A fragrance was there, strong and clear. And here it is again, now even stronger. You recognize it, but you can't place it. It's more than just a scent, a perfume . . . the perfume of a flower . . . a pungent, troubling flower, but you can't remember what it looks like or even its color.

Leaning over your open book, you attempt to continue reading. But the sweet perfume slides between your eyes and the words, dancing like a reflection on water.

You decide that you have to clear this up. Your nose leads you, nostrils quivering, along the trail. The scent is hard to follow. It appears, only to disappear just as fast. It's playing games with you. But little by little, you direct yourself toward the source.

There it is. The bouquet in the vase. That's where it's coming from. A combination of white petals and the leaves of the lilac. Delighted, you approach it. What a disappointment! It's not that one. Not exactly. A bit irritated, you continue your search. You go through the rooms one by one. In the somber office, you discover, beside the window, against the light, a bushy plant with shiny, almost black leaves. But it has nothing to do with the gentle scent you seek.

Just before closing the door, neverthless, something makes you retrace your steps. Nestled between two leaves, it appears, newly opened. Its fleshy petals, white as snow, are still crumpled. This is the one that sent the first vibrant call that pierced your soul, this is the one, the desired, the awaited, the gardenia!

Silence

The songs of the birds wake you in the morning. Or more precisely, one bird's song, a long, warbled, solitary song. A song for no reason, for no one.

You might as well get up. Rays of light dance in the cold room as you clear your throat, just to hear the sound of your own voice.

Around you is only silence.

You think about the town in the distance. Sometimes the house seems completely quiet, but it only last two or three seconds, at the most. It's like a wave that surges back, leaving the beach smooth and serene, in the space of just a few seconds—a random pause in traffic, movement, and words. Suddenly people, expressions, houses filled with people, are revealed, and noises that are normally inaudible, like the sounds of the garden, flow toward you.

Here, in this house, is only silence. Thus you should hear and see everything. But your ears are clumsy, your view fogged. Not only do you not hear or see anything, but you bump into furniture, trip over yourself, become irritated. Everything seems too close, too heavy, too cumbersome.

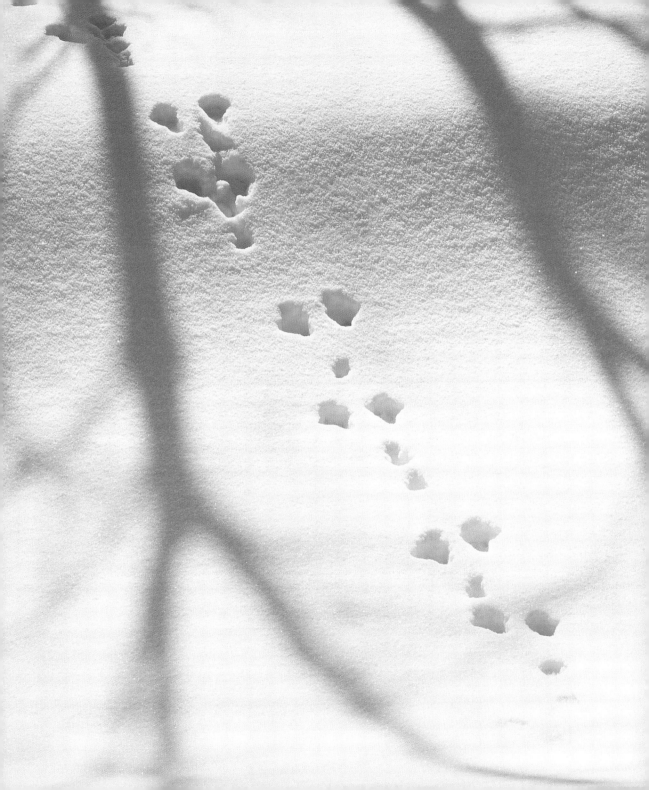

Feverish, agitated, that's what you are. The opposite of relaxed. You slept poorly last night. The sound of your own heart invaded the room, because of the silence.

Silence, what is silence?

If you ask the question, the answer you'll hear is, "When there isn't any noise."

The absence of noise—that's the theory. But silence is something else, beyond the absence of something.

One time you heard silence, real silence.

Was it the Khafre or the Khufu pyramid? You can't remember anymore! However, you do know that you climbed, heart beating furiously, alone with the guide, on a steeply angled passage into the core of the pyramid. Twenty times you hesitated, legs like rubber, overcome with panic.

What were you afraid of?

Silence, just silence.

A silence like you have never heard. Yes, heard. This is a silence you can hear. It can even be deafening, almost like never-ending thunder. It's a silence that echoes your own silence, which you have silenced within yourself.

What you learn as you penetrate deeper into this tangible silence is that it has a thickness, a texture, and a depth; it dwells within us but never shows itself to us under normal circumstances, never lets itself be heard through the everyday noise.

You were made of silence, and you were about to discover that, and that's what scared you.

Be silent and see what comes to the surface: silence and more silence. An expansion of silence, and silence that expands, stretching until it is more vast than all of the nights in the universe.

That's what you glimpsed.

Silence is not an absence; it doesn't exist merely by default, like space in a cell that exists only because it's surrounded by four walls. Silence is dynamic, a real presence, an existence; it holds energy and sense.

It is not simply a lack of communication. No. It is a life, a reason to live.

Silence is within us.

The steps scraping under your feet, the movement of the clock, once again make themselves heard in this new day. Your ear is becoming more fine-tuned and sensitive. It registers the finest difference in sounds, just as the finger senses different words in braille. There are echoing

spaces, dull places, places where sound rises, others where it falls, some
that breathe in, others that push out . . . for those who want to hear it,
there is the relieving sound of silence.

You knew that voluntary periods of silence could be beneficial, but
standing here on the threshold of silence, you begin to understand
its real significance.

Why were you so afraid?

What were you afraid of hearing?

Your own voice? That of the shadows? Cries of anguish, screams
of terror, scolding, evil spells, horrible moaning? Smothered
words, things you don't want to hear, deep, dark secrets revealed?

People who never stop talking are afraid of silence. Those who
have the radio and the television permanently blaring fill and
cover up their own silence. They are afraid to find themselves
before an empty, depopulated zone, about to fall in.

So between themselves and the world, these people put up bridges
of noise that they can hold on to, and constantly strengthen it with
new phrases, new noises, and new words that, even if they are devoid
of sense, keep them from falling into what they believe is just
emptiness.

But there is no emptiness.

There is silence. And this silence, they don't know what it is anymore; we don't even know what it is anymore.

Sitting before a steaming cup of coffee, while slowly buttering your toast, you try to let silence play its game.

Silence could be a laugh that suddenly bursts out from your throat, shaking you in a liberating spasm. Silence could be one word, just one word, or even an idea that comes from nowhere, from the deepest part of your mind, or from anywhere—why not?—just as a bird lands on a branch. Silence can be an image, a memory, a sudden desire. . . .

"I will speak only in the presence of my silence."

Let's try it—to speak only in the presence of our silence.

It's a strange notion. But let's try it all the same.

Your mouth opens, then closes again. You have nothing to say. That's normal, because silence . . . no, that's not it. It's your tangible silence that you feel within yourself. Simply speaking, in this silence, words become rare, even nonexistent. At least at first. You don't know what to do with this silence. You feel awkward with it.

Silence is not some kind of monster, because it is within us, it is part of us; but it is a part of us that we are not familiar with, so there is a hint of strangeness about it. If we let it have its way, silence soothes our thoughts, it fills our spirit. As incense spreads in a room, it unfolds into all surrounding space. Barriers built by words fall, bridges melt, roads are erased, the landscape is once again wild, pure, beaten by the winds . . . it becomes a land where, here and there, signs emerge that are part of a new language, a new way of life.

Speaking in the presence of silence, you can stop the word games—the silly back-and-forth between people, the rogue waves that cause interference in the communication of silence to silence. These trivial words, which seem more like noise than sense.

It is necessary to come to terms with this silence, within yourself and outside yourself. And to do this, you must stop the game of interactions.

Silence allows you to extend your hearing and listening—beyond the field of your ears, beyond your entire self, beyond other, beyond the confines of the world.

Whereas noise shrivels you up and makes you recoil, silence teaches you expansion of thought and of the body. Deep thought once again becomes acquainted with language. Words anchor themselves in the earth of silence and push their colored stems toward the sky.

Music

A sonata spreads out in the room, familiar. Sometimes it sounds distant, according to the whim of the movements of the house. You half listen to it, but you know it by heart, it's been so long. From time to time, your own voice emphasizes a chord, accompanies it, like a counterpoint . . . then abandons it, because you're already someplace else. This melody is like a too-familiar face; you no longer know its contours, and the spirit of it escapes you. At its base it is a pleasant sound, a finished music canvas, and you think it can bring nothing new to you.

But while you're preoccupied with something else, suddenly there's a chord—you suddenly imagine a pianist's hands arched over the keys, his body tense, his breathing even—that recaptures your attention. It's the first time you've ever noticed it. The first time? How could you have been listening to this melody up until now, and did you know how to really appreciate it?

Listen! Immediately you settle in a comfortable position, away from anything that could prevent you from listening carefully. In a back room, in a big armchair, you sit with everything that could augment your listening experience within arm's reach: a comforting drink, a smooth cigar, a window opened over the garden.

You have to know how to give yourself up to the music. You have to put yourself in a position to welcome it and make yourself available to it. To feel filled with the resonances of music is not an easy thing. You must accept the blossoming of unknown sensations and forgotten emotions that ring in a new way within you.

Beyond the choice of music itself—it must be by instinct—to choose a melody and let yourself be carried away by it is to force yourself down a secret path of your soul. It is vital to develop keenness of listening.

Solitude

You were just talking to yourself.

Yes, you were. No use denying it. You heard your own voice echoing in the big living room. Anyway, it's not the first time.

Sometimes you talk to yourself in a sort of inner monologue: you encourage yourself, you congratulate yourself, you joke with yourself. Sometimes you address yourself as a kind of superior, to whom you must stand up, and prove yourself; to whom you address particularly colorful tirades and offer unanswerable arguments. Of course, in these you are always absolutely correct. You, the solitary orator.

And all of this happens as you're strolling around, naturally. Because, let's not forget, you are a normal person, even though you talk to yourself, even though people who talk to themselves make children giggle, like some kind of clown with a sad face uttering silly musings. It makes the little ones laugh, albeit nervously.

Up until now, you've never known solitude. You've occasionally glimpsed it as it approached you, forcing you to spin a hundred and eighty degrees to avoid it; you've also crossed paths with solitude at other people's houses, without wanting to meet it at all.

You've always feared it, in a way. Isolation, rejection, entrenchment, emptiness, nothingness, fear . . . this is how you imagine solitude, with a capital S, something that makes you hit your head against the wall.

Here, in this house, there has been nothing but solitude. Let's say that this is the time for solitude, that you are conducting a solitude experiment.

Even if it's no big thing, even if it offers you only a glimpse, a mechanism has been switched on.

The fact of being alone, speaking to no one, having no person to answer to, affects the way you perceive your place in the world.

Imagine! Normally, days pass by in a series of coming and goings, based on feedback with the outside world. It's always, "I extend my hand, you extend yours, we reach each other and hold on." "I smile at you, you smile at me, or maybe you don't, but you answer me anyway" "I talk to you, you talk to me, we talk together." "I touch you, you hug me, we hold each other tight." The other person is there, with his thoughts, his physical self, sending us real, concrete, physical perceptions. All this allows me to determine my outer limits, to check them, to permanently situate them so that I know where I stand with them, where I am, what place I take in the world, how significant I am.

The absence of contact, whether it be by word or by touch—you just almost squeezed your own hand to feel your own body, as if for the first time—makes your outer limits a little more fluid. Your flood of thoughts slows down—this is the reason why you've caught yourself talking to yourself vehemently—words ramble, and movements lose their pertinence.

It seems—and this is undoubtedly part of the process of finding solitude—that an off-centering takes place, a slip from the point or zone from which you normally work out your perception of the world and of yourself in this world. Here, displaced, you feel a floating sensation as you lose all sense of reference points, and a hesitation creeps into each of your thoughts and acts.

But this feeling can only be transitory; deep down, you know that solitude is more than just a floating feeling. Austerity, a sort of grandeur, emerges from the three syllables of the word. You even begin to be aware of a certain clarity, a precision of contours, to such an extent that just pronouncing the word causes you to straighten your collar, hold yourself more correctly.

So what is solitude? Something serious that expresses itself as a posture or an attitude. Why is it that when we bring to mind the idea of solitude, it seems to be, all at the same time, close yet distant, friend yet enemy, human yet inhuman, a dream yet also a fear?

Undoubtedly it's because it speaks of another self—another self that is found outside you, outside your vain egocentrism. It's this other self that we experience during this displacement, this off-centering: something that is you, but held away from you, that is where you can find solitude.

Solitude is your shadow cast on the ground, which is simultaneously attached to you and outside you, a separate image, yet an intimate projection of yourself. If you are ever afraid of it, it's because it makes you move out from your center, forces you to go beyond your limits, and thus compels you to look at yourself, the world, and yourself within the world in a different way.

This is how you feel things. Hold yourself at the outer edge of yourself; that is, separate yourself from mere sensations and feelings and come back to a more concrete place, so that you can actually push against that wall, as you are doing right now, pushing against the wall of the garden. Here you are, not exactly inside, but not completely outside either.

You have a different look about you. You can now internalize passions, but you've also embraced the horizon of the outside world; you accept intimacy but are in touch with the world outside your domain. You are pushed to always love and know yourself but to also to love the world, and thus to reintegrate yourself in it.

The greatest thing about solitude is this detachment.

The floating feeling has dissipated, replaced by something you would call lucidity, maybe another way of saying solitude.

In this precious space, illusions do not last long, and you cannot hide, mask, or paint over your true face. Everything is open. There's no need to show off, either. You are simply there, impoverished yet enriched.

Boredom

When was the last time?

During adolescence? Later? Before?

Hard to say.

All you know is that you have no trouble recognizing boredom: a dark and dirty mist that, in the space of a few seconds, obscures all thought and throws a view of mourning over everything.

Nothing—not the garden, not the milky sky, not the roses—can dissolve this mist. The things that, only yesterday, you found enchanting, today you find unbearable.

You felt it coming on this morning, before you even opened your eyes. It was hidden in your sleep, already infusing your dreams, just waiting for the moment you put your feet on the floor to get out of bed so that it could completely submerge you.

Maybe that's why you hesitated to get up. With a heavy body and a numb spirit, you tried to postpone this moment, but then it was time to face the fact that boredom, taciturn and morose boredom, had come to visit you.

You almost laughed at first because, up until now, you thought you were immune: "I am proud to say that I am never bored!" Insinuation: I have so many resources, I have so many strings to my bow, so many possibilities just waiting to be discovered, that it is impossible that boredom—that is, that I should no longer know what to do or that I should lose the desire to do anything—can affect me.

In the event of boredom, you had, up until now, plenty of diverse activities to occupy you, and many excellent reasons to devote yourself to them. Any situation can trigger a bout of boredom— a dinner, a reception, an event, a family or social obligation. . . .

Immediately, like a false friend, you try to reverse this feeling, you find a good reason to accept that you must be there, you push boredom, kicking and screaming, out the door.

"On Sundays, children are bored," sang Charles Tenet. It's true that as a child you experienced boredom. On certain occasions, your discomfort took on the form of sickening stickiness, suffering away the afternoon in your great-aunt's dim, old-fashioned living room ("Of course, we'd love to visit!") while between the closed shutters you glimpsed the blue sky; spending time on homework during vacation; Sunday dinners; obligatory naps. . . . Ah, the torture that extinguished the fire inside you . . .

But now it's something else. Nobody is obliging you to do anything, yet there emerges an intimate, intrinsic boredom; it seems to come from your very depths, but up until now you had fended it off.

You were about to utter the fatal words, "I'm bored," in the whiny, disillusioned tone of a child who spins around in circles and then collapses; you recognize this gloomy way of being because you've already experienced it before.

The mirror reflects a nasty face—vicious, even.

What is happening? Who are you mad at? At those who are unable to distract you from your boredom? At those who are not bored, despite their lack of activity? At the whole world, certainly.

You knew that boredom could come at any time—you predicted it!—but it came so fast, and it came in disguise, so you weren't prepared for it. While you were in the process of doing nothing, you opened wide the door to idleness, so you shouldn't pretend to be surprised.

Let's resolve to resist boredom, to be stronger than it, to combat this invader.

And to do this, you must look at yourself straight in the mirror, the only witness to your determination, and urge yourself to take action.

But it seems useless: in your features you see the same lethargy, and in your eyes, the decision that you made a few seconds ago is already wilting, like a flower deprived of water.

Okay.

Maybe you were too strict with yourself. You need to be more subtle, more clever; you need to develop a strategy. Step by step, you are going to push boredom out of your domain, but without attacking it head-on, lest once again the impulse simply to "do" take hold.

Let's try it. You start by attempting to sort through your books, but before you've finished, your shoulders slump, and a deep sigh overcomes you.

No, it's useless to continue; your heart just isn't in it. There is really and truly nothing you can do.

You collapse in an armchair, discouraged, drained of energy.

The sound of the clock's pendulum begins to infuriate you. You won't wind it anymore; that will shut it up. Your limbs feel unusually weary, and in your mouth is the taste of dirt. You take a good look around you, but nothing, absolutely nothing, captures your attention. The world has nothing to say to you, communication has been cut off, and you know that even if your dearest friend instantly appeared in this room, his presence would give you no pleasure.

"Bored to death!" The expression is not an exaggeration. Do you really know what boredom is when you've never experienced it?

You know that up until now, you have fought it with all your strength. You feel now that your energy is close to zero. You are alive, yes, but barely. To desire nothing, to feel only distaste for everything—that is not life.

You need movement, joy, desires. And here, you are running on empty. None of your ideas or desires, which normally make you leap, or at least smile, or, in one word, react; nothing distracts you from this boredom. Dozing off is out of the question: even closing your eyes bores you!

Boredom is like those insatiable black holes in the skies that have the capacity to absorb everything: body, energy, light. Everything that approaches, everything that normally arouses your interest, is immediately absorbed by it. Everything is drained of its meaning: desire, need, beauty, whim, curiosity, greed. . . .

You know that you've always struggled against boredom. When you felt it rising in you, slow and brackish like brown water, you braced yourself against it, full of the energy of despair. It was the enemy to defeat. You devoted yourself to impulsive acts, work, sports, shopping. . . . So what did you fear?

In asking yourself this question, you begin to feel your defenses fall. You have always been afraid of boredom, as if it's something that will dissolve you, weaken your foundations, but maybe you were wrong. Were you perhaps just afraid of a part of yourself?

This boredom that you felt break through this morning, which has by now completely infected you . . . what if it is a sign, a signal emitted from your very depths? What you feel rise to the surface is a calm zone, as in the deep sea, where everything moves slowly. A space where no desire, no project, not even something relaxing, pleasing, or free of worry, can come to disrupt you.

It's an obscure force, unreal and slow. This feeling is worrying at first because your will, determination, and reason have no place. You must learn to let yourself go, let yourself be carried away.

To know how to be bored requires, paradoxically, courage; you can't be afraid to go toward the emptiness, the slowness, the unexpected. You will find there, if you let yourself go a little, a tranquillity that gives rise to dreams free from the demands of a world always in movement.

Tension is released, the winds subside, your thoughts finally calm, nothing causes you worry; and your body, relieved, refreshed, finally finds its inner peace.

Laziness

A long, very long sigh, "a declaration of no worries" as Alain once wrote, is proof of your drowsiness; you finish it with a blissful smile.

How good it feels! You never realized how comfortable and soft this bed is. Your hand, sliding between the mattress and the bed frame, confirms it. Here, everything is wool, linen, and quilted. Not to mention the fluffy eiderdown, so thick that it takes up a good part of the room and whose old-fashioned appearance normally would irritate you; you usually prefer, Spartan style, your practical, crude woolen blanket.

"O laziness, take pity in our long misery! O laziness, mother of the arts and of noble virtues, you are the balm for human anguish."
Paul Lafargue

But this afternoon, you do not shun this pleasure. It must be after noon by now, and you've barely moved since this morning. Just one short trip to the kitchen to bring back a tray of buttered toast, a steaming cup of coffee, and a thermos for refills, and then you dive right back under the warm sheets, without a book, without anything at all, the lights switched off, with simply the shutters open to a neutral, unmoving, quilted sky.

Until now, breakfast in bed was your declared enemy, a symbol of indolence and idleness; you spent all of your existence avoiding anything that resembled lethargy, languor, slothfulness, or, in general,

carelessness. Brought up to be obsessed with the fear of laziness, a voracious and cynical monster that conjures up images of decrepitude, decay, even degeneration, you always kept it at a distance for fear of a total and irreversible collapse.

Inertia and the state of being horizontal, two things that are inextricably linked, seem completely incompatible with a life founded on principles of work, activity, and the spirit of enterprise.

"The early bird catches the worm." How many times have you heard this adage, when all you wanted to do was prolong your slumber? Apathy, irresponsibility, sluggishness, immaturity, thoughtlessness, these are the terms associated with lazy people or with those who risk becoming lazy.

For those who are committed to "doing," the presence of lazy people, or even their mere existence, is absolutely unbearable. How can you take anyone seriously who, instead of "giving all they've got," lives in an exasperating state of nonchalance? Worse than just provokers, the lazy are accused of undermining, even wearing down, the foundations of existence.

All that the active person bases his life on is completely ignored by the lazy. Exactness, order, politeness, clearness, activity, memory, these are just some of the rules that he abides by, but these rules aren't absolute laws to be blindly followed. Meanwhile, at the boundaries, at the limits, the lazy escape with the ease and silence of garden snakes, smoothly and discreetly. Basically, the moment that they are needed, they disappear, slipping between your fingers.

If obligations find only an echo inside the lazy, it's because time for them doesn't have the same value as it does for others. While we are constantly running after time, the lazy person has already seized it, has invested in it a true power, a personal dimension, bestowing it a presence, a depth, a reality, that those who are constantly on the run are completely unaware of.

To confront laziness is not an easy thing. Its critics never accomplish their goal. It's as if an invisible force field deflects even the most acerbic movements, curses, arguments, and remarks, protecting he who, collapsed on the sofa at three in the afternoon, seems to ignore the world that buzzes around him. Whether you attack him straight on or at an angle, nicely or with a little rudeness, the lazy person answers you with an understanding smile out of consideration for all of your efforts, but he won't move one iota.

Nothing can force him out of this laziness—not moral arguments, not a sense of duty, not family or social obligations. The lazy person gets around these situations, preferring "to do nothing at all rather than to do something poorly." The lazy person doesn't owe anything to anyone.

To complicate things, the lazy are generally good-humored, and that is their weak point. The irritation and scorn of their detractors doubles at the sight of the merry indifference with which the lazy receive their criticism.

The lazy seem happy, and that's the problem. They don't experience any suffering or any bad moods. They do not have a guilty conscience. They truly, frankly enjoy the present moment, without reservation, anxiety, or melodrama; with lightness and with freedom from worry, with vitality.

And that's what you're experiencing today, by pulling up the sheets under your chin and stretching out your legs voluptuously in the cool, crisp, unexplored depths of the bed. A half-eaten piece of toast scoffs at you from the night table, but you don't touch it because you're not going to clean up anything today. Even yesterday's mess, which normally would have made you jump out of bed, ready to clean it up, doesn't disturb you.

Anything that has been long forbidden eventually becomes a secret and powerful desire. Who hasn't envied the passive force of the lazy? Who has never dreamed of such freedom from worry? Of such simplicity of the soul? Of such freedom to simplify one's existence? Why get dressed if you're not going out? Why work so much if a little is enough? What attracts us to laziness is the freedom it allows us to separate ourselves, to disconnect from all that the world adheres to, without the least amount of self-criticism. What do the lazy say? They say, "All that you believe is fundamentally, necessarily, absolutely important does not matter to me. I not only ignore your values and the way you idolize them, but I turn my back on them."

You must have courage to embrace laziness. It even requires a certain enlightenment, a certain higher perspective, to have the power to demand it and live it. That's why the lazy person is bothersome, and why others flee from contact with him: viewed from the lazy person's perspective, all of their projects, desires, brilliant deeds, and enthusiasm deflate like a pierced balloon.

By taking the time to explore laziness, as you have done today, you realize that you have a lot to gain.

First of all, a little flexibility. Your book isn't finished? You have one last errand to run? You absolutely have to make lunch? In general, you're the one imposing these tasks on yourself, grumbling all the while. Meanwhile you can just as easily leave certain things for the next day; instead of making these things into obstacles, think of them as a new chance at continuity, a new blossoming.

You will also find that the value of your time is modified. For those who run from one thing to the next, laziness allows you first to slow down and thus to taste and to make the most of each seized moment before finally going deeper into what it is. Existence is no longer a race, a rush to get ahead; someone has cried out, "Stop there! Let's all stop, enjoy this present moment, because this is where it is happening, and not elsewhere." "Elsewhere" and the future don't exist from the lazy point of view. It's the here and the now that count. There are no regrets and no hopes. Free will, because there is free will—even extreme determination—is practiced, here and now.

You begin to take this laziness a bit more seriously. Isn't this the attitude of someone in a healthy mental state? Someone who is capable of opening up to laziness, isn't that someone who courageously obeys the need to deeply enjoy the moment? Isn't it a way of resisting, of refusing to fit the mold, of not allowing your wings to be clipped?

Could it be that laziness is the art of unfolding a lounge chair while ignoring those who critique you? Maybe!

Suddenly, you admire the lazy. You love them. You also love the part of you that you felt growing, the part of you that you repressed each time it tried to express itself and that, up until now, kept you from enjoying each instant, each fleeting moment of life.

The Dressing Gown

*"To move forward
meant shaking free his
dressing gown not only
from his shoulders,
but also from his soul
and spirit."*
Ivan Goncharov,
Oblomov

For those who want to familiarize themselves with laziness, the
dressing gown is the gentlest of teachers. More than an article of
clothing, it's a manner of being—just as the emblem on a riding
boot suggests conquering activity, the dressing gown suggests its
diametric opposite. The best way to approach the dressing gown
is to take a bath or a hot shower, perfume yourself lightly, and
slide over toward it, taking care to leave your skin naked.

The choice of dressing gown is important—that goes without
saying. Often the oldest and most outdated is the best. You recall
with emotion your old soft silken robe, purple-hued with a
black velvet collar, whose softness was incomparable. . . . The
dressing gown knows how to keep its promises; its charm takes

effect immediately. From the moment that you gently adjust the tie around the waist, you experience a strange sensation of lightness, as if this article of clothing absorbs all of the tensions caught up in your body and expels them, cleansing you of them, in one magical gesture. Awaking in you passionate secrets by way of this game of caressing, light contact, the dressing gown pulls us toward the bed, the armchair, or the sofa, and you regret not having one of each in every room.

Incense, steaming tea, the scent of roses flowing toward you, a beloved book slid between your fingers, the curtains brushing gently along the ground; nothing exists except the exquisite pleasure of this forgotten time of the past and of the future.

Idleness

A man of leisure, a bird, idleness.

Flapping wings, elegant and graceful movement, a caress, a winding road free of unforeseeable detours stretching out before you . . . is this idleness?

Setting out for an early-morning walk, the wind in your hair, hands in your pockets, strolling around according to your whim, you happily experience for the first time the feeling of giving in completely to your own desires.

Idleness is such a curious state of the soul. How can you recognize it? By a certain detachment. By a certain desire to break free from everyday activity, to hold yourself at a distance, as if places and objects cannot hold you down anymore, as if they no longer have the ability to tie you down; you feel the need to pull up the anchor, to let yourself experience an adventure, without worrying what you're leaving back on earth, but also without any specific goal in mind.

Detached, yes. Furniture, walls, hedges, you have left behind, eager for air, space, emptiness. The faint sweet smell of the lime trees calls you, and so do the soft breeze that rustles the leaves and the immense, blue

sky, clean and fresh, like an open invitation to let go.

It's almost as if the quality of your outlook and your consideration of the world has changed. You've given yourself some distance, of course, but some elevation as well. Your point of view is no longer the same, and the horizon you embrace is larger, vaster, revealing perspectives unknown to you before this moment. You feel like a bird.

What feeling are you experiencing? You don't feel especially lazy, although you don't feel inclined to start any major projects either. This is a state of opening up, of availability, where all of your faculties are receptive to your inspirations. To be curious, accessible, ready to react: that is being idle.

Indeed, to be idle, you have to be able to fulfill the dictated requirements: follow the laws of instinct, randomness, spontaneity. You must not abide by a plan, nor have any purpose.

So, you've left the house without any idea of what time you will return, without even knowing if you will return. To those who ask you, you say that you don't know, and more importantly, you don't want to know.

What is so wonderful about this is that before you a horizon stretches with no boundaries, where all obstacles and borders have been erased. When you were a child, the immense beaches on the coast of the Atlantic fascinated you; what a pleasure it was to walk along the beach, knowing that it would never end. You walked for the sole purpose of walking, and that in itself made you so happy that you thought you would never need or desire anything more.

But without doubt, idleness goes hand in hand with childhood. The consciousness of a child is not a completely blank slate, of course, because it has already been immersed in thousands of sensations and impressions, but it's not as compartmentalized and rigid as that of an adult, either.

The consciousness of an idle person has the lightness and hypersensitivity of that of a child. Doors are open, passageways are free of obstacles, and communication is made easy. Everything that grabs your attention interests and amuses you.

Idleness makes you open, an observer, curious. You open your arms to other beings, events, and things without discrimination. They are all stored in your consciousness, accessible to your sense of curiosity. The idle person chooses a path, explores it to the end, only to abandon it for another. The straightest route isn't without its problems, so he selects his road arbitrarily.

His wanderings aren't unlike those of a bird who dives toward the earth to grab something but then at the last moment swoops back up toward the sky, letting himself be taken by the wind, gliding in the cool currents, soaring upward towards the warmth; he is really living, with his wings unfolded, completely available to any situations that the outside world may bring him.

That's why idle people scare the rest of the world, who are not used to

thinking outside the box. You never know where they're going, what they're doing, or what they're trying to accomplish. They never take on any precise project, they don't stick to the plan; they just follow their noses, at the whim of their inspiration and intuitions, without any concern that their only boss is their own free will.

It's true that idlers have their bad points. You think that they are ready to try anything, eager for new and unplanned experiences. But the idle actually have the habit of taking roads backward, disappearing from here and then reappearing somewhere else, and they are never there when you are waiting for them. They're always in the wrong place at the wrong time.

The idle have nothing to prove, and that is what's so infuriating. It means that they have nothing to show, to explain, or to justify. Their choices are based on what things are worth and what these things will bring to them, not on what they represent. What matters for them are experience, curiosity, discovery.

The idle cannot be forced to fit the mold. They are too evasive, too much in love with their liberty and freedom from worry. You can accuse them of being superficial, you can talk about their instability or their inability to stay still, but except for those who really take advantage of being idlers—those who choose not to work and to leech off of others—this is not true; in general, idleness undoubtedly does good by giving those with an open spirit the capacity to appreciate the savor of existence.

Strolling around, you begin to wonder if you are even capable of capturing this idleness that you feel ripening deep inside you; it could be a useful lesson for mastering the art of doing nothing. Sure enough, little by little a path appears in the road. By following your impressions, you begin to realize that all of the micro-events making up this day form not only a logical and rational whole, but a kind of branching tree that enables you to perceive the world more widely, in a more flexible manner.

Intuition, if it is well managed, is a major asset in the life of an idler, and if there was one and only one path to take, it would be this one. Intuition is what allows you to progress, guided by chance and curiosity, in the spirit of listening and being receptive to things that otherwise couldn't make themselves known to you.

To that extent, idleness is beautiful. It assures an open, permanently awake consciousness, molded by many impressions and opportunities. You can also think of idleness as a period of apprenticeship, but the purpose is not to learn a certain skill for once and for all; it is to learn a skill that can be used again and again whenever you need it.

As soon as your life seems to be escaping from the boxes you've tried to put it in, as soon as you feel rigidity and an absence of vision setting in, provoking all the nightmare scenarios you've ever imagined, you should embrace idleness.

Here is a way you can unclog the system, and reconsider the world around you from a lighter and fresher outlook. By welcoming in this open state of mind, you can both give yourself distance from that which weighs you down, and restore lightness to all things.

Today you definitely feel that by introducing idleness into the moral and aesthetic scope of your existence, by reconsidering it, by looking at it from a different angle, you have realized that it can be useful for you.

To hold on to your idle spirit (that is, to keep it in an open state, receptive, awake, and not to weigh it down with preconceptions) is to nourish and enrich it without prejudice so that, when the right time comes, you can once again find idleness as soon as you need it.

The Armchair

You chose it carefully. It was difficult, because in addition to being comfortable, it had to be aesthetically pleasing. The criteria were: luxurious material, pure lines, excellent comfort so that you could completely relax. You didn't want to make a mistake. Choosing such a chair is a project, a commitment. Right away when you saw it, you knew it was the one because of the shiver down your spine, but just to check, and to be sure that this sensation wasn't merely a fruit of your overactive imagination, you came back again and again to look at it. It was the one.

The reason why you were so demanding is because you remembered the lounge chair in the sanatorium in Thomas Mann's novel *The Magic Mountain*; it was more than just a functional chair, it was a symbol. Besides its utilitarian functions, it offered a sense of timelessness to those who rested on it.

What you wanted was difficult to define: you wanted the armchair to relieve you of the weight of your own body; you wanted to feel its arms embracing you, its seat lifting you off the ground; you wanted it to disconnect you from all that usually supports you and from your everyday tension. You wanted this armchair to establish intimate communication with the poles of your body and, through this dialogue, offer you long-awaited rest.

Daydream

A thought loosens and frees itself from your depths. Slowly and softly, it leaps from your slumber.

Like a bubble, it swells and expands in a daydream that calmly invades your consciousness and the abstract of the real world.

Where are you?

"Daydream, seeing the present as favorable images, belongs to femininity."
Gaston Bachelard

Maybe you are lying down in a little boat. Stretched out on your back, your head resting on the edge, you slowly drift on calm waters that seem to exhale the sweet scents of mint and gorse; soothed, your eyes open wide to take in the slowly whirling sky, to follow the drifting clouds. The calm rustle of leaves, as if the trees above you are breathing, expands and grows stronger. Shadow and light, warmth and freshness . . .

How long have you been daydreaming? You can't say. Reverie took hold of you while you were squatting on the wooden pontoon, fascinated by the progression of a water spider, revolving in this exact spot where the river covers the base of the soft and fine silt where chips of minerals sparkle.

You climbed aboard the unsteady boat, enveloped in the warm odor of

fresh tar; you put the paddles in place, stashed fishing gear under the seat, and from the moment you untied the cord, you felt the river really take hold of you.

Quickly, the riverbank disappeared, landmarks were erased, and the dock vanished behind the thickness of the alders. You've just embarked on a voyage to a dreamlike landscape detached from the outside world, where all traces of civilization have disappeared. Only the occasional sound of an animal diving, or of birdsong like crystal chimes in the trees, confirm the presence of life.

Under the soothing influence of water, visions surface that completely transform your perception of the world; fields of wheat spring up from the waters, golden reeds rustle under the sun; a tree, bowing toward the river, laps up a drink with its leaves; the long hair of water nymphs that inhabit the world below wave greenly below the surface, blocking the path of the boat, forcing you to lean over and ponder the depths.

Who inhabits the river? There was a time when you would have been haunted by the strange creatures you invented in your own mind. But today, this river seems on the contrary not to conceal any other mystery but to be everywhere the same. It is only an exact, infinite repetition of molecules, like microscopic planets, these bodies that attract and repel each other according to immutable laws, which to the naked eye, because of the oblique rays of the light as they push back the limits of the shade, appears to you as liquid matter. Infinite brilliant bodies, like dust, like infinitely small stars, dark stars . . .

So the river carries you. It takes you away from your earthly self, and awakens in you all that is feminine, dreamy, open, and supple. It carries you on its flat back, with its vast and slow force, careful not to interrupt your dreams. And little by little you feel soothed, lighter, detached from the things that weigh you down, floating on the surface of yourself, relieved from all the burdens and cares that up until now blocked the blossoming of your dreams.

What are you dreaming about? You can't say, because your dreams have been so intertwined with reality. This experience infinitely exceeds what your spirit thought possible; you feel peaceful, happy, light. It is a daydream in its purest state. On the surface of reality, this pleasure opens up, widens, and comes to nourish this immense dream that lives within you.

At times you've tried to contemplate a dying fire or the calm sea at daybreak, but nothing compares to this heart-to-heart with the river, this dialogue with your soul.

A branch brushes lightly against your face. You are once again conscious of the lapping sound of the water. The river is in high spirits. It runs. Sitting up straight, you seize the oar and plunge it into the water's depths. A red and white float, forgotten by a fisherman, dances on the water's surface. A dragonfly with glittering blue wings lands on the edge of the boat.

The world floats back to you. A child waves to you, clutching a butterfly net. A fish leaps out of the water. In your hands the wooden paddles help you listen to the secret music of the river, the river that

speaks, the river that gives birth to dreams.

Reverie brings necessary rest to the soul, where tension tries to dominate.

You distance yourself from the river, leaving your dreams behind, knowing that you have found a path leading to relaxation; a relaxation that is not that of sleep, not that of immobility, but stems from a calm, expanding presence within, the presence of plentitude.

How long has it been since you let yourself succumb to reverie? Not since childhood, certainly, where it reigned as master. What does it matter! Reverie is a place that we always dreamed of going, not knowing if it really existed or not. Now we know that it's not so far away. With a little effort, a little detachment, we can find it again.

Become Yourself

"The art of doing nothing? You're talking to the right person! Yes, you could say that it interests me!"

How many of us, just thinking about doing nothing, let out a sigh of relief? The desire to do nothing is in all of us. It is one of the necessary aspects of our vital energy, a natural counterbalance to our tendency to be overactive.

We all have this need—even those who work themselves silly; maybe they even more than the others. What are they fighting against, those who drown themselves in activity and who avoid silence and stillness at all costs, if it's not the mild, gentle, serene part of themselves? What are they afraid of, if it's not the fear of being absorbed by it?

By viewing life as a struggle or a battle, you end up being your own worst enemy.

To do nothing requires a lot of courage. It's not a question of walking around in a daze, waiting for something magical to happen to you. "Doing nothing" is breaking your habits, questioning yourself, finding new places to dock, accepting that there is more than one way to look at the world, and considering things under different angles.

It's about letting go. You must start by looking with a critical eye at a fast-paced lifestyle, with emphasis on performance and efficiency at all costs; you must fully grasp reality by experiencing the moment, the senses, values, tastes, savors, and perfumes.

Doing nothing does not require that you abandon your living, active forces. On the contrary, you should rediscover your activities but not let them become dissolved in stress, tension, and animosity.

It is a matter of giving yourself the chance to sail, to float, and to drift on the immense floods of consciousness so that you can experience the vigor and vitality that is inside you. And for that, it is necessary to give up a certain amount of control, of domination, and of the constraint that emanates not only from the world surrounding you but also from within you.

To practice the art of doing nothing is to dare to plunge down to your very depths so that you can rise higher than before, even higher than your dreams of superiority and control could ever take you.

Thus can you hope to become finally and fully yourself, in this constant exchange between action and rest, this balancing act between the need to control the world and the desire for the power of reverie, between reality and dreams.

PHOTOGRAPHY CREDITS